PRICING FOR PROFITABILITY AND GROWTH

Mastering Pricing Strategies for Technology and Services Globally

Stephan S. Sunn

Davidson Global Partners, LLC

Copyright © 2024 Stephan S. Sunn

©Copyright 2024 -2026 Stephan Sunn All Rights Reserved

Disclaimer:

This book may not be reproduced or transmitted in any form without the written permission of the authors. Every effort has been made to make this guide as complete and accurate as possible. Although the authors have prepared this guide with the greatest of care, and have made every effort to ensure its accuracy, we assume no responsibility or liability for errors, inaccuracies, or omissions. Before you begin, check with the appropriate authorities to ensure compliance with all laws and regulations. Every effort has been made to make this report as complete and accurate as possible. However, there may be mistakes in typography or content. Also, this report contains information on online marketing and technology only up to the publishing date. Therefore, this report should be used as a guide – not as the ultimate source of Internet marketing information. The purpose of this report is to educate. The authors do not warrant that the information contained in this report is fully complete and shall not be responsible for any errors or omissions. The authors shall have neither liability nor responsibility to any person or entity concerning any loss or damage caused or alleged to be caused directly or indirectly by this report, nor do we make any claims or promises of our ability to generate income by using any of this information.

Davidsons Global Associates & Co. LLC, Davidson, NC 28036, USA; All Inquiries of copyrights, and cooperation go to: Stephan.sunn@aya.yale.edu

CONTENTS

Title Page
Copyright
Preface
Chapter 1: The Pricing Paradigm Beyond Costs
Chapter 2: Know "Why" Behind Each Pricing
Chapter 3: Pricing Intelligence
Chapter 4: Mastering Value-Added Pricing Strategies
Chapter 5: The Art of Closing Deal at Right Price
Chapter 6: Currency Fluctuations and Market Variations
Chapter 7: Aligning Sales, Marketing & Pricing
Chapter 8: Dynamic Pricing via Data-Driven Analytics
Chapter 9: Eight Pricing Strategy Errors to Avoid
Chapter 10: Critical Takeaways and Future Trends
Acknowledgement
About The Author
Books By This Author

PREFACE

The author and his partners contributing to this series of professional guidance and industry best practices possess over two decades of experience advising multinational corporations and C-suite executives. They are esteemed thought leaders within their respective fields and globally renowned throughout their extensive professional networks. Prior to the COVID-19 pandemic, when international travel was unencumbered, they would convene annually at a rotating global location. Their first reunion following that worldwide crisis was imbued with a profound sense of gratitude for having endured such a cataclysmic event.

Reuniting with one another brought joy to all of us. Even more so, the notion of how delicate and short life began to settle in. The idea of documenting our business experience and lessons, successes or failures, to help our colleagues and clients was formed in 2022 when we gathered in Jamaica. However, with the arrival of ChatGPT and similar trailblazing AI technologies in late 2022, this small proposal gains urgency because we fear within the next decade these revolutionary technologies could transform our lives and society forever, and resemble what COVID-19 has brought to us.

The subject matter of this book series are the business domains we have supported clients worldwide last two decades, with the priority in the last few years. We don't claim we are the researchers or professors in the technologies, but the practitioners who evaluate, choose, and apply state-of-the-art technologies to solve business problems. The technology breakthroughs are not what we pursued, the critical criterion is if the technology solved the business problems with business values. This is why

"Case Studies", "Examples" or "Lessons" are weighted much higher than the rigorous analytics of the theories in these business guides.

This book dives into advanced pricing for tech and service businesses. It argues for setting prices based on customer value, not just cost. Understanding customer needs and market trends are crucial. For complex solutions, the book explores "value stacking" to price each element based on its impact.

Competitive intelligence and strategic positioning are also covered, along with pricing models like subscriptions and freemium. Upselling and cross-selling are included to maximize customer value. The book offers a decision process of intelligent pricing to win more deals.

CHAPTER 1: THE PRICING PARADIGM BEYOND COSTS

In the quickly changing world of technology and services, the traditional cost-plus pricing methods of the past are increasingly ineffective. This manner of pricing only considers the cost of production and then applies a markup. In this approach, there is no consideration of the value that the innovative, technology-enabled solutions deliver to our customers. This is resulting in companies leaving money on the table and fighting for their lives in an ever-rapidly evolving market.

In the tech sector, nothing exposes the limitations of cost-plus pricing quite like the value of a product or service that resides in realms well beyond the tangible. Consider, for example, the software solution that saves its users thousands of hours of working time each year by automating what was a very manual operation. The value shown in the product and service's prices should be more than mere development price plus a certain profit margin.

Furthermore, cost-plus pricing does not take into account the different requirements and worth sentiments of different client classes. With some buyers willing to pay top dollar for cutting-edge features and personalized service and others focusing on simplicity and low cost, one-size-fits-all pricing no longer can cover it.

Fortunately, another solution exists, value-based pricing. This approach places the customer at the heart of pricing decisions by setting prices based on the value of the good or service to the customer, not just on its cost of production. By tying prices to the distinctive benefits and outcomes achieved by your offering, you'll be able to capture a greater proportion of the value you create and develop stronger, more profitable relationships with your customers.

In order to begin value pricing, a business must first gain an extensive understanding of its target customer. This includes carrying out comprehensive market research, segmenting customers, and examining data to discover the important aspects that cause the customers of each customer subgroup to buy. By knowing how each buyer uses the product or service, the results the buyer achieves from it, and the choices the buyer has among alternative products and services, one can achieve a more detailed idea of an accurate evaluation of the price one should charge for the product or service.

Now that you know this, you can develop a value proposition that speaks to each of these client groups and spells out the measurable benefits of your solution in language that resonates with your customers. It may mean emphasizing expense savings, productivity improvements, higher quality design—or whatever outcomes matter most to your clients.

After you've gotten the definition down, the next step is to quantify your value proposition in monetary terms. This is problematic with intangible benefits, like improved customer satisfaction and increased brand loyalty. However, you can build the case for the financial impact of your offering—and thus, your pricing strategy—by utilizing customer surveys, case studies, and ROI calculators.

Naturally, pricing based on value is not something you do once and forget about. When market conditions change and new competitive factors emerge, a company's decision-makers need to continually re-evaluate the present pricing strategy to ensure that it is still aligned with customer value perceptions and business objectives. If not, a change is necessary and pressing. This requires a flexible, data-driven process that enables you to quickly respond to new opportunities and challenges.

The hard work of prescribing value-based pricing will be discussed in the coming chapters. We will cover getting into the market and segmenting your customers to develop powerful pricing strategies that can communicate your value signal. By adopting this new thinking and placing the customer in control of your price, you also develop your company into a competitor in new technology era.

CHAPTER 2: KNOW "WHY" BEHIND EACH PRICING

How to Define Your Value Proposition: A Recipe for Uniqueness and Selling Success

In order to effectively implement value-based pricing, you must first possess a clear understanding of your unique value proposition (UVP). Your UVP forms the foundation of your pricing strategy since it serves as the vehicle for which you convey the specific benefits and outcomes that your technology or service offering delivers to the buyer.

Begin by determining the main attributes and capacities of your solution that separate it from competitors. These could be characteristics like performance, dependability, user experience and support. Next, convert these features into concrete benefits for your clients. For instance, if your solution runs 10 times faster than competitors, this sets the stage for increased productivity.

To focus on the outcomes that are most important to your target market, you should collect and analyze customer data. Interview, survey, and do focus groups with your customers to find out what they consider to be pain points, goals, and priority items. Use this information to craft a compelling value proposition that speaks to their specific needs and wants.

Measuring the Value of Your Customers' Experience: Converting Benefits to Business Impact

After you describe your proposal of value, the following stride is advancing your proposal quantitatively in expressions your customers can without much of a stretch follow and grasp. This suggests translating the difference your provision will make into money, such as expense funds boosting, income-generating, or working more competently.

To do that, you need to gather data on the current costs and performance metrics of your target market. This may involve looking at industry benchmarks, talking to existing clients about the problems and costs that your product would alleviate, or using ROI calculators to estimate the potential impact your solution would have plus what it would take to get there.

If your software, for example, helps clients automate a manual process that currently takes 10 hours per week, you can calculate the annual cost savings based on the average hourly wage of the employees involved. Similarly, if your service helps clients increase sales by 10%, you can estimate the additional revenue generated over a specific timeframe.

When you communicate the worth of your product or service in specific, quantifiable terms, you strengthen your case for your pricing model and help customers understand the true value of your offer.

Topic Spotlight: Utilizing Value Stacking for Intricate Technology Solutions

When companies offer complex technology solutions that have many components or modules, it is especially difficult to measure the value to the customer. In these situations, the concept of value stacking becomes particularly important.

Value stacking is the process of breaking down your solution into its individual components and determining the value that it delivers to the customer. By giving a specific value to each component based on its contribution to the overall business impact, you can paint a better picture of your solution's worth.

To illustrate, think of a customer relationship management (CRM) platform that has sales automation, marketing automation, and customer support modules. Each module might have several different benefits. Sales automation promises to ramp up sales team productivity. Marketing automation promises to increase conversion rates. Customer support might lead to improved customer satisfaction. By quantifying the value of each module one by one, you can show how your solution adds up, and with that comes to a higher price.

In addition, value stacking provides an opportunity to develop pricing packages that correspond to different customer groups so their unique requirements and preferences are taken into account. In doing so, you can propose multiple combinations of modules or features at different price levels to arrange your pricing strategies in line with profitability requirements and with respect to the value you offer to the target customers.

When you're rolling out value-based pricing at your company, keep in mind that the key to success is all about understanding and communicating the unique value that your technology or service promises to your target market. By taking the time to define, quantify, and stack your value proposition, you can craft a pricing strategy that actually captures the real return that your product delivers — and distinguishes you from the competition.

CHAPTER 3: PRICING INTELLIGENCE

Comprehending the Competitive Landscape

In a world of rapidly changing technology and services, prices don't exist in a vacuum. To construct the most effective pricing strategy, you have to intimately know your competitive landscape – the pricing models, value propositions, and market positions of your key rivals.

To begin, you should locate your direct and indirect competitors, both from your own industry and from adjacent markets that provide similar or substitute goods. Collect data on their pricing strategies, including list prices, discounts, bundling options and other value-added services they provide.

After that, review how your competition positions itself in the market. Do they push for premium pricing, calling attention to the distinct features and benefits of their product? Or do they make pricing simple, going after price-conscious customers with plain, get-the-job-done offerings? Knowing these position strategies can help you identify holes or openings in the market your pricing approach can take advantage of.

Also critical, you should be keeping tabs on competitors' marketing and sales tactics. How are they communicating the value proposition to potential customers? What channels do they use to reach their target audience? By knowing how they are approaching these activities, you can gather meaningful insights to help you best showcase the worth of your solution and justify the amount you're charging/commissioning.

Strategic Placement for Financial Gains: High-end vs. Low-price Costing Approaches

Once you've developed a strong comprehension of your competitive landscape, the next thing you need to do is figure out how to position your pricing approach optimally. The two most popular options are premium pricing and value pricing.

A premium pricing strategy involves setting your prices higher than your competitors, based on the unique or superior value that your technology or service delivers. This approach is particularly successful for companies that have a strong brand reputation, innovative features, or exceptional customer support. By emphasizing the added value or exclusive benefits of your offering, you can attract customers who are willing to pay more for quality and differentiation.

Conversely, value pricing emphasizes delivering a superior solution at a more affordable price than your competitors. This methodology is directed toward customers who are more price-sensitive and are looking for the most value for their money. By operationalizing your organization, rationalizing your cost structure, and ascertaining economies of scale, even though keep prices competitive you will still be able to sustain profitability.

To succeed with either approach, you must ensure that your value proposition is clearly communicated and distinct from those of your rivals. You must be able to express the specific benefits and outcomes—the "why and wherefore"—that your solution delivers to your target customer, whether your positioning is as a premium provider or as a value leader.

Exclusive Analysis: The "Freemium" Approach to Technology and Services

A pricing strategy that has become more popular lately in the technology and service industries is called "freemium." The way it works is companies give away a "lite" version of a product or service for free, then charge for additional features, functionality, or support.

Attracting new customers and establishing brand recognition can be accomplished in a very useful manner through the freemium model. The ability to demo the value of your solution, coupled with low barriers to entry, empowers potential clients to experience firsthand what they'd be buying. By offering a limited yet handy version of your solution to customers for free, you can rapidly increase the size of your user base while also gathering valuable data regarding customer behavior and preferences.

Despite that, the freemium model has a few cautiously suggested hazards and difficulties that may be incurred. This model could cause potentially higher customer acquisition prices, conversion rates are possible to be diminished, and possibly, a struggle to monetize your user screen to generate a profit. To really prevail while using the freemium model you must be armed with a strong up-selling and cross-selling plan for your premium features along with a deep grasp of the lifetime value of your customers.

When considering whether a freemium model is right for your product or service, you need to be thoughtful about your target market, the competitive landscape, and your business plan. By assessing the potential pros and cons of this model, you can decide whether or not it is in line with your overall pricing plan and value proposition.

Keep in mind that the top objective of your pricing strategy is to make as much money as possible while also giving your customers the value they want. In order to do this successfully, you have to get comfortable with competitive intelligence and positioning. It's also critical to know your ideal customer's buying power and consider the market for your products. Remember that it's a juggling act: you have to balance your revenue goals with what the market will bear.

CHAPTER 4: MASTERING VALUE-ADDED PRICING STRATEGIES

Create Value Bundles That Sell

In today's competitive technology and service markets, merely setting a base price for your offering may not be enough to maximize profitability and attract customers. There is a powerful way to enhance your pricing strategy – Bundling. Bundle multiple products, services, or features into a single, value-packed offer.

Bundling gives you the ability to create different and better packages that match the distinct requirements and wishes of each market segment you target. Just as importantly, by putting together those 'right' components you can raise your proposition's perceived value and command a higher price than could be garnered for each item selling on its own.

Let's take, for instance, the case of a software firm. It may offer as part of its main product various add-on elements that are related, such as extra data analysis components, customization capabilities and a higher level of support. By packaging all of these components together, the software firm is able to broaden its appeal to customers in search of a more all-inclusive solution – customers who, in turn, are, by the way, often prepared to pay more for the convenience and the added functionality.

Before crafting your bundling strategy, it is crucial that you take into account each customer segment's unique value drivers and pain points. By conducting market research and analyzing customer data, you can pinpoint the combination of products, services, and features that are most likely to resonate with each segment and generate the highest levels of adoption and revenue.

Subscription pricing refers to a pricing strategy in which customers are charged a recurring fee to gain continuous access to a product or service.

Subscription pricing models have steadily become the norm in the software-as-a-service (SaaS) industry, but over the past decade, companies in a myriad of industries have started to offer products and services to customers on a subscription basis... Restricting entry to paying customers is really not the biggest goal of the strategy. The biggest goal is to turn traditionally one-time customer purchases into ongoing revenue streams.

Subscription-based pricing is a pricing model that is becoming more and more popular in the technology and service industries. Under this model, instead of making a one-time purchase, customers pay a recurring fee (usually monthly or annually) to access your product/service.

There are several key benefits to subscription-based pricing, for both companies and customers. First, subscribing to a software suite lets the customer use what they need for a shorter amount of time. Second, subscribing to a software suite offers a financial benefit for the customer, by only paying for what they use. Finally, subscribing to a software suite offers a financial benefit for the company, knowing the number of subscribers lets the company know the software is worth continuing, or if enough time has passed, updating.

Subscription-based pricing is frequently more flexible and provides superior value than one-time purchasing. Your customers can split your solution's cost into smaller payments to make it accessible and affordable. Even better, subscriptions often come with updates, upgrades, and support, so you will always have access to the latest and greatest features!

If you are considering the use of a subscription pricing strategy, then you need to attend to how you structure your offers. Elements such as contract length, payment frequency, and cancellation policies all affect customer adoption and retention. Once you are underway, you should use customer feedback, market demand, and competition to continually experiment with prices.

The Technique of Increasing Sales and Expanding Marketable Products

Upselling and cross-selling are two powerful techniques to help optimize the value of your customer relationships— just like bundling and subscription-based pricing. Upselling is encouraging a customer to buy a more expensive version of the product or service being purchased. It could be a higher tier (and price) or something with more features/benefits included. Cross-selling is suggesting (to the customer) that they consider purchasing a related or ancillary product or service in addition to what they came to buy to help improve or extend the value of the customer's original purchase.

To effectively upsell and cross-sell, you'll need to be able to put yourself in your customers' shoes. You'll need to understand their needs, preferences, and behaviors. By analyzing data on their purchase history, usage patterns, and feedback, you'll be able to recommend additional products or services to them in a targeted and personal way that adds value to their experience.

For instance, if one of your customers has been using your company's basic software package for several months, and has consistently been bumping into built-in usage limits, you might reach out to offer an upgrade to a premium plan with higher capacity and additional features. Similarly, if a customer has already purchased your core product, you could recommend a complementary offering or add-on that will help them achieve their goals faster, more effectively, or more efficiently.

To be successful in upselling and cross-selling, focus on the customer's needs and the value they will receive from the offer rather than only aiming for higher sales. By providing personalized, timely, and relevant offers businesses can create trust and loyalty with customers while pushing incremental revenue and profitability.

When putting together your value-added pricing strategies you should keep in mind that the goal is to create a win-win situation for both your business and your customers. By continuously investigating new avenues for bundling, packaging, and delivering your offerings in ways that maximize value and convenience, you can differentiate yourself from the competition and create loyal, sustainable, and lucrative relationships with your target market.

CHAPTER 5: THE ART OF CLOSING DEAL AT RIGHT PRICE

Getting Ready to Negotiate Successfully

Pricing successfully in technology and service industries often means negotiating with prospective customers, particularly for high-value or complex deals. Getting the best results requires going into each negotiation well-prepared and with a clear game plan.

Begin by conducting extensive research into your customer's company, industry, and particular needs. Discover the customer's primary pain points, objectives, and criteria when making decisions, and think about the extent to which what you are offering can meet the three of these factors differently. And then by using this intelligence, adjust your selling recommendation— as well as the price — to better match your particular situation and concerns.

Additionally, forecast possible sales resistance criteria and come up with the answers and responses in advance. Frequently, possible sales resistances or sales criteria will embody budget constraints, other competitive offerings, and ROI distrust. By proactively designing your counterarguments and evidence to speak to each of these potential objections, you'll maintain your credibility.

It is also important to clearly define objectives and limits for negotiations. Your ideal price point should be determined, as well as the minimum threshold you are willing to accept, based on your costs, margin goals, and broader business objectives. A clear definition of your bottom line helps you make decisions with full information, and avoid agreement to terms that may ultimately compromise your profitability and long-term success.

Understanding Pricing Psychology: Anchor and Frame Your Offers

Effective negotiation goes beyond planning. Additionally, it requires a knowledge of the psychological theories that shape people's decisions and perspectives. First, two major ideas to absorb are anchoring and framing.

The concept of anchoring initially and most prominently appeared in a 1974 research paper written by Amos Tversky and Daniel Kahneman: "Judgement Under Uncertainty: Heuristics and Biases". Anchoring is a cognitive bias and acts as a decision-making heuristic in which an individual depends heavily on the first piece of information received. The first piece (anchor) presented to an individual influences their perception of the following information. The term anchoring describes the process of fastening an idea or concept in a person's mind. The concept suggests that people make adjustments from any reference point. The anchor can be arbitrary and unrelated but can still have a huge effect on any questions that need numerical estimation. Many experiments can be conducted to test the anchoring effect.

However, this paper will be more focused on anchoring in pricing. Typically, most economists would say the price has gone away by the fact they make no profit in a competitive market therefore price made not a whole lot of difference. Many consumers today would say they pay whatever is worth the product because they need the product and they also believe they know how much the product should be worth. But it does turn out that the first offer does have a significant impact on the willingness-to-pay of customers, especially those all aspects sound equal. In other words, it is common for people to ask "how the price" before even asking "what the product". Consequently, anchoring in pricing needs to start from the beginning of the price presentation.

To use anchoring to your advantage, think about initiating the negotiation with a higher initial price than your ideal target. This might create a more positive reference point and make later offers look more reasonable in comparison. But be careful not to raise your anchor too high; doing so might discourage the customer from participating at all.

Framing, however, means presenting your pricing and value proposition in a way that highlights the benefits and outcomes that matter most to the customer. By choosing your words carefully, and by emphasizing the specific ways in which your offering addresses the customer's needs and priorities, you can shape the customer's perception of value—to the point where your higher price is actually justified.

For instance, instead of only stating your price, you could frame it in terms of the cost savings, revenue growth, or competitive advantage that your solution can provide over a specific time period. By quantifying the tangible impact of your offering and presenting it in a relevant, compelling manner, you can make a stronger case for your value and increase the likelihood of a successful close.

Sealing the Agreement with Certainty

Closing a deal at the right price is often a matter of confidence as well as incorporating a level of persistence into your negotiation techniques. By properly preparing, and effectively anchoring and framing, you'll be able to close a deal. Having those things will help bring you closer to those goals.

There is one tactic that can be useful and it comes to using silence effectively. In presenting your offer or responding to a question, after you are done speaking, just sit there in complete silence. Give the other person time to process and respond rather than rushing to fill up the silence. It creates some heaviness and some importance and then makes them maybe ponder, "Wow! This is something really worth considering."

A further element that is essential for a successful close has to do with knowing when to walk away. If the customer refuses to meet your minimum price threshold or insists on terms that would compromise your ability to deliver value, it may be necessary to politely but firmly decline the deal. By being willing to say no to unfavorable agreements, you can protect your long-term interests and your reputation, while signaling to the market that you are convinced of the value of your offering.

At the end of the day, developing discipline in order to negotiate pricing involves blending preparedness, psychology, and persuasion. By deeply understanding your customer's desires and hot buttons, translating your value proposition into terms relevant and engaging to them, and staying poised and principled throughout, you can reliably close deals at prices that reflect the actual worth of your technology or service offering.

While perfecting your negotiation skills and tactics, keep in mind that the objective is not merely to optimize immediate returns but to foster long-standing and mutually profitable relationships with your clients. By greeting every negotiation as a means to design value and navigate problems mutually rather than as a confrontation, you can establish trust, allegiance, and support that will serve your organization well into the future.

CHAPTER 6: CURRENCY FLUCTUATIONS AND MARKET VARIATIONS

Comprehending the Pricing Landscape on a Global Scale

In the modern age of increasing global interconnectivity, many companies that operate as technology developers and service providers encompass entire areas of the globe in their customer bases. This occurrence can present extraordinary opportunities to achieve exponential and often rapid growth and expansion, but it also poses a number of particular challenges and difficulties when it comes to setting pricing and determining pricing strategy.

Currency fluctuation is one of the most important considerations in global pricing. Exchange rates can fluctuate enormously over time, shaped by economic, political, and market forces beyond your control. Fluctuations like these can have a very serious effect on pricing, margins and competitive position in different markets.

In order to be able to cope with these rapidly changing circumstances, you should first: build a comprehensive understanding of different currency exchange rates together with economic situations across destination countries; check currency volatility frequently; and develop alternative strategies to accommodate dramatic fluctuations.

A key part of global pricing is seeing how local markets work and what customers there want. In each country, rivals, rules, culture, and spending power skew the way customers think about a product.

In order to thrive in this intricate context, it is necessary to perform in-depth market research and analysis for every region you are targeting. Dedicate time to recognize the primary competitors in each market, understand their pricing and positioning in the market, and evaluate how your product's offering compares to their product in terms of features, benefits, and value proposition. Use this approach to get all data and information to build specific pricing strategies that are in accordance with what customers from your selected markets expect and need.

Optimizing Cost Structures: Constructing Adaptability for Worldwide Pricing

There is another essential part of international pricing for companies that goes hand in hand with understanding market dynamics: optimizing your cost structure. By running a tight ship and keeping strategic options open in your operations, you can be better able to adapt to changing market conditions and maintain profitability across regions. For instance, if you are going into a high-cost country like Japan, you might need to cut costs elsewhere or change your operations to require fewer resources, so you can absorb that country's costs.

Begin by completing a comprehensive examination of your present price configuration, involving the unchangeable bills as well as non-unchangeable disbursements. Discover subdivisions where there may be an occasion to abridge overhead or amplify perfection, such as revolutionizing manufacturing routines, discussing excellent provisions with dealers, or mechanizing definite performances.

Next, think about how you can inject a greater amount of flexibility into your pricing and packaging. One way to do this might be through modular or customizable solutions that permit customers to select only the specific features and capabilities they require, rather than a one-size-fits-all offering. This can help you better fuse your pricing with the unique needs and budgets of customers in different markets.

Another technique to consider is to introduce dynamic pricing models that autonomously change in relation to real-time market conditions and demand. By employing data and analytics to consistently optimize your pricing, you can be confident you are continuously capturing maximum value for your solution while staying competitive in every market.

Exclusive Report: Transfer Pricing in Global Business

When dealing with various branches in different countries, an organization must consider transfer pricing in their pricing strategy. Transfer pricing refers to the price that a company charges particular units in the corporation for goods, services or intellectual property to move up, down or across.

Transfer pricing is heavily regulated and scrutinized by tax authorities in many countries to transparently reflect the true economic activities and substance of these intercompany transactions to accurately generate taxable profits in each jurisdiction. In order to avoid costly penalties, not to mention reputational and legal risk, organizations must establish, document and maintain solid, defensible, arm's length transfer prices that meet the standards set forth by tax authorities around the world.

When you set prices for the transfer, you must consider multiple factors such as the exchange good or service's value, the market circumstances in the location, and the overall of each subordinate revenue. You must cooperate with the IRS and legal law experts to ensure your work is to fit, the guard and the compare strategy with your general business strategy.

If you are proactive and deal directly with transfer pricing as part of your global pricing strategy, you can reduce your risks, optimize your tax position and make sure that your pricing practices are uniform and equitable throughout all regions and entities.

As you make your way through the intricacies of global pricing, remember that getting it right requires a judicious mix of market savvy, operational dexterity, and strategic alignment. By keeping a constant finger on the pulse of changing market conditions, honing your cost structure, and adapting your pricing and packaging to appeal to specific customers in each region, you can build a powerful, lasting pricing strategy that fuels growth and profitability around the world.

CHAPTER 7: ALIGNING SALES, MARKETING & PRICING

Internal alignment: The triumvirate for pricing strategies

In order to successfully implement and execute a value-based pricing strategy, a strong alignment and collaboration among your sales, marketing, and pricing teams is critical. These three functions combine to form a powerful triumvirate that must work seamlessly together to communicate your value proposition, engage your customers, and drive profitable growth.

Begin by encouraging transparency and sharing of information among the teams. Hold regular cross-functional meetings, where each department can share updates, insights, or best practices related to the evolving, competitive dynamics of customer needs and market trends. Do this consistently, and it will safeguard that each person is working from the same lenses of your targeted market, value return, and sales planning.

Next, define clear roles and responsibilities for each team in supporting your pricing strategy. Your marketing team should handle building persuasive messaging and content that explains your unique value proposition and separates you from competitors. This might include case studies, whitepapers, webinars, and other thought leadership materials that show the tangible impact and ROI of your solution.

Conversely, your sales crew should have the requisite resources, training, and encouragement to convey your value proposal to prospective buyers and tackle price dialogues with certainty. This may include standardizing pricing models, objection handling guides, and value calculators that gauge the benefit of your product in a way that aligns with the individual customer's corresponding needs and priorities.

In conclusion, your pricing team must be in tight collaboration with both sales and marketing to consistently test and enrich your pricing strategy based on marketplace feedback, competitive intelligence, and performance data. This will likely require you to modify your pricing model, packaging options, or promotional tactics in order to be more in tune with customers' preferences and willingness to pay, all the while ensuring your capture of a fair share of the value you create.

Marketing to Add Value to Products

To develop a value culture, external communication and understanding of value are paramount, in addition to the creation of internal alignment. Your marketing team is key to structuring the way prospective customers understand and appreciate the value of your technology or service offering.

In order to market for value perception effectively, the first step is to gain a deep understanding of your target audience and their unique needs, challenges, and goals. Conduct market research, customer interviews, and data analysis to discover the key value drivers and pain points that your offering addresses, and use this insight to create messages and positioning that resonate with each segment of your audience.

Additionally, concentrate on generating content and campaigns that inform potential clients about the complete range and consequences of your proposal. Forsake just spotlights traits and profit attributes, and alternatively stresses the perceptible results and consequences that your solution can support them to accomplish. Utilize these case studies, testimonials, and successful stories to exhibit how your offering accomplishes ascertainable consistency and ROI for businesses alike. You should use different platforms and approaches to impact and captivate your specific audience group using digital marketing, occasions, establishing your brand as a thought leader, and vital alliances. By, ensuring the value you have to offer is visible through a mixed format and variation of touchpoints to help create attitudes of identification, respect, reliability, and quality.

Enabling Sales to Sell on Value

Ultimately, the success of your value-based pricing strategy depends on your sales team's ability to convincingly communicate and defend your value proposition in real-world customer conversations and negotiations. To support this critical function, we recommend investing in ongoing sales enablement and training initiatives that equip your team with the skills, knowledge, and tools they need to excel.

First, give extensive training on your value proposition, pricing model, and key competitive advantages. Make sure each person on your sales team can confidently and consistently articulate the unique benefits and outcomes that your product or service provides, as well as its relative superiority to alternative options on the market.

Then, establish a solid collection of sales encouragement materials and sources that uphold value-centered exchanges and contracts. Examples are modifiable pitch deck materials, ROI calculators, illustrations of how you can make life better, how to debate, etc.

Lastly, create an environment of consistent learning and improvement amongst your sales group. Promote education sharing, exchange of best practices, and peer-to-peer coaching, and enjoy ongoing training and development programs to better the skills of sales team members and be adaptable to shifting market conditions. By investing in the continued growth and success of your sales team, you can develop a formidable value-based selling engine that will fuel long-term revenue growth.

As you strive to develop a value culture throughout your organization, remember that alignment, communication, and enablement are enduring endeavors that necessitate persistent exertion and care. You can form a value creation and capture flywheel that drives sustainable, profitable growth for your business by cultivating strong collaboration between your sales, marketing, and pricing teams and constantly tweaking your approach based on customer input and performance metrics.

CHAPTER 8: DYNAMIC PRICING VIA DATA-DRIVEN ANALYTICS

Harnessing Big Data to Optimize Pricing

As technology and services continue to evolve at a quick pace, conventional pricing models are being replaced by more dynamic, data-driven options. Organizations now possess the power of big data and advanced analytical techniques to gain access to real-time insights into customer behaviors, market trends, and competitive dynamics. Armed with this knowledge, companies will be able to optimize their pricing strategies continuously with the goal of driving the greatest impact and profitability.

First, you'll need to identify the key data sources and metrics most relevant to your pricing decisions. This might include internal data, such as sales history, customer demographics, or product usage, as well as external data, like market trends, competitor pricing, and economic indicators. Bringing together and analyzing these diverse datasets will give you a more complete view of the factors influencing demand and willingness to pay for your offering.

Additionally, think about getting advanced analytics solutions -- platforms and tools that can help you sift through all this information and give you good advice for when it comes to actually - DO something about it all. For instance, machine learning algorithms can analyze customer behavior to identify patterns and correlations, predictive models can forecast future demand and revenue, and optimization engines can adjust prices on the fly in response to changing market conditions.

When you adopt a data-focused process in relation to pricing, you are empowering yourself with the knowledge and self-assurance to prioritize your commercial objectives and make decisions that make sense to your customers. The potential for maximum revenue, market share, or profitability can be measured through a big-picture/big-data perspective.

Experimenting with price, also known as A/B testing or price experimentation, has become increasingly important for companies in any industry. With the rise of data-driven decision-making, companies need insights into how price changes can affect their bottom line and whether they can charge higher prices to increase revenue. In order for a company to experiment with price, two different prices must be shown to two groups of people, and changes in demand must be tracked. In other words, companies want to know if they can sell more or less at higher or lower prices.

There can be a lot of different methods as to how people are selected to see a different price, for example, a website may choose some of its users to pay a different price. Factors that could determine which users see which price, could be things like cookie size, IP address, time of day, a user's location, etc. Anything that the website can use as a randomizing element will work to ensure that the only difference between these two groups is the price that they see.

Another powerful technique to optimize your pricing strategy is performing A/B tests and price experiments. This involves creating multiple versions of your pricing and packaging and randomly exposing them to different segments of your customer base. By doing this, you can quantify their effect on key metrics such as conversion rates, revenue, and customer lifetime value.

When you are ready to begin A/B testing, the place to start is determining which components of your pricing to test. Consider factors like your base price, any discount levels, different bundling options, or pricing tiers. Create variations of each element, making certain to keep all other factors the same to accurately measure the change's impact.

After that, distribute each version randomly for a percentage of the audience that you are targeting, and in a set amount of time observe their behavior and abstract the outcomes. Based on a statistical analysis select the best-performing version using the essential metrics and apply it across your whole customer base.

Experimenting with price can also help you test more radical or innovative pricing models, like pay-per-use, subscription-based, or outcome-based pricing. You can gather important data and learnings that will help you inform your long-term pricing strategy by piloting these approaches with a small group of customers and carefully measuring their impact.

Achieving success with A/B testing and price experimentation boils down to starting small, iterating quickly, and being prepared to fail fast. Through ongoing tests and optimizations to your pricing, you can develop a more agile and customer-centric approach that adjusts to evolving market dynamics and consumer preferences armed with real-world data and feedback.

Pricing in the Future: AI and Machine Learning

In the near future, AI and machine learning are likely to be the key weapons as companies try to improve pricing in technology and services. The two technologies will be able to change the pricing in two ways: first, they will be able to provide adequate decision-making with support from a large amount of data and complex algorithm automatically, secondly, they will be able to get more results even from existing data.

To illustrate, AI-driven pricing models are able to examine vast amounts of data from diverse locations on a continuous basis. With this information, models can detect connections and trends that would undoubtedly remain hidden from human eyes. They can then make changes to pricing based on fast-paced inputs including customer sentiment and competitor behaviors. As a result, businesses can be at the forefront of current developments, demonstrating flexibility and driving their pricing strategies for the greatest effect and potential to gain profit.

Additionally, machine learning algorithms can apply dynamic pricing strategies that are more personalized to individual customers by tailoring pricing to the particular and unique needs as well as preferences of customers. These algorithms are able to effectively anticipate a customer's will to spend by analyzing their past buying, browsing, as well as demographic data. They can suggest tailoring the price to fit a specific customer, looking after relationship management and revenue management when dealing with the customers.

As AI and machine learning mature, business leaders need to stay ahead of the curve by leading organizations to look for venues where these technologies can be integrated into pricing strategies. This may require that they hire some new talent, partner with specialist vendors and service providers, and develop a culture of ongoing experimentation and innovation.

At the same time, it is crucial to approach these technologies with a clear understanding of their limitations and potential risks because AI and machine learning models are only as good as the data they are trained on, and can be susceptible to bias, overfitting, and other pitfalls if not properly designed and validated. As a result, it is essential to have human expertise and oversight involved in the development and deployment of these systems, as well as to continuously monitor and adjust them based on real-world feedback and results.

By adopting artificial intelligence and machine learning in a prudent and deliberate manner, enterprises may unlock rich veins of efficiency, agility, and competitiveness in their pricing approaches. In an era where technology and service industries continue to advance relentlessly, individuals capable of wielding these instruments and techniques will be well-positioned to capture opportunities in the swift and data-laden pricing futures.

CHAPTER 9: EIGHT PRICING STRATEGY ERRORS TO AVOID

Pricing is an essential element in any winning business strategy, but it's also a complex and difficult task. Whether it's the lack of accurate data, the difficulty of aligning all the moving parts (sales, marketing, c-suite), or just the challenge of adapting to change, pricing mistakes can have a huge impact on a company's bottom line and long-term success.

We'll examine eight of the most frequent errors in pricing strategies in this chapter, in addition to offering sensible advice on how to avoid or conquer them.

Mistake 1: One of the most basic pricing mistakes companies make is their failure to understand the perceived value of their products from their customers' point of view. Failing to understand why customers are willing (or unwilling) to pay gets companies into trouble by causing them either to set prices too high (and alienate potential buyers) or to set prices too low (and therefore cut into profits in a big way).

To avoid this, it is important to conduct extensive market research and to do a very careful job of customer segmentation. In parallel, firms must build a deep understanding of the specific needs, wants, and value drivers of each target segment. Among the tools that may be used are conjoint analysis, customer surveys, and focus groups, combined with analysis of historical purchase behavior and demographics.

Mistake 2: Overlooking Competitor Behavior and Responses: Another pricing pitfall is neglecting to consider competitors' behavior and responses. In today's highly competitive technology and service markets, monitoring competitive moves and then adjusting pricing and ancillary strategies accordingly is a continuous and never-ending process.

This does not imply engaging in some sort of bone-headed race to the bottom on price but simply knowing exactly what value you uniquely create and how you position it relative to your competitors. By tracking competitor prices, promotions, product introductions, and back-counting the cost of materials out of existing list prices, you can see potential threats and opportunities coming miles away and trigger your own commands to keep an offering compelling and differentiated.

Mistake 3: Depend Too Much on Cost-Plus Pricing: Cost-plus pricing could be a good starting point for price setting; it is seldom the most productive or profitable route in the long run. If a company charges only a fixed markup to production costs, it may fail to capture the full value of its offerings or react to altered market conditions.

Instead, think about implementing value-based pricing strategies that connect the prices you charge with how much customers believe what you sell is worth and the benefit they'll enjoy from buying it. That could mean using methods such as conjoint analysis, economic-cost-value estimation, competitive benchmarking, and a philosophy of trying different pricing models and packages to see which one works best.

Mistake 4: Failing to Take the Psychology of Pricing into Account Pricing is about more than just economics—it's about psychology too. How prices are framed, displayed, and communicated can have a profound influence on customer perception and behavior, even if the intrinsic value of the offering remains constant.

In order to take advantage of the psychology of pricing, think about anchor pricing (starting out with a high price to make other offers appear more reasonable), charm pricing (using prices ending in .99 or .9 to imply a good deal) or decoy pricing (displaying an ugly option to make other options look more attractive). By knowing and using these ideas, you can cause clients to accomplish what you want and then some.

Mistake 5: Failing to segment and differentiate Pricing is an inherently individual exercise; one price does not fit all. Different customer segments have different needs, wants, and propensities to pay. Failure to understand and respond to these differences is a failure of pricing that leads to suboptimal prices and lost opportunity.

To prevent this mistake, think about creating different pricing layers, packages, or groups that reflect the individual preferences and value appraisals of each targeted part. This can include offering numerous feature sets, service levels, or pricing models determined by features like the representative's size, activity, or usage case. By providing a wider choice of options and price spots, you can seize a greater part of society and improve revenue and profit.

Mistake 6: Failing to Recognize the Primacy of Timing Pricing is everything, and failing to address the temporal dimensions of customer behavior and market dynamics can result in big missed opportunities or lost revenue. For example, launching a new product or service at the wrong moment (e.g., during a recession or around Christmas) can sharply limit its uptake and success, while neglecting to adjust prices in line with changing costs or demand can steadily erode margins and competitiveness over time.

To ensure optimal timing of your pricing strategies, there are a number of considerations to keep in mind. These can be loosely broken down into three categories: seasonal trends, business cycles, and customer buying patterns. Some examples of matching your pricing strategy to these cycles include techniques such as:

- Dynamic pricing: The price of your products is adjusted in real-time as a function of supply and demand.
- Time-limited promotions: Discounts for a limited period of time to encourage an immediate purchase, as the customer waits longer their willingness to pay gradually reduces.
- Subscription-based models: Set a flat rate price regardless of the quantity of products/services you receive, allowing you to spread your decision-making in terms of purchasing throughout the entire year. This strategy even outs the cash flow throughout the year.

By aligning your pricing with the natural rhythms and cycles of your market, you can ensure that your strategies will have maximum impact and effectiveness.

Mistake 7: Failing to Recognize the Value of Transparency and Communication Customers can be very sensitive, and sometimes emotional when it comes to pricing. Not being clear on your pricing changes and policies, or not communicating them at all, can therefore lead to lots of confusion, frustration, and potentially even some backlash. When social media and online reviews are getting common even popular, it's incredibly important for companies to be upfront and proactive in communicating, even sharing, your pricing strategy with customers. Customers' feedback, positive or negative, is important to approve or disapprove pricing strategies.

One way you could do this is by providing well-organized billing specifics on your website or flyers, creating reasons or briefings for pricing changes or differences, or communicating with clients directly to address their needs and concerns. With transparency and open communication, you can reassure and secure your clients even though some difficult pricing decisions are being made.

Mistake 8: Neglecting To Stay Updated And Flexible: Lastly, a very typical and expensive pricing mistake is a failure to continuously monitor and adapt pricing to changing market and customer conditions. In fast-paced and dynamic technology and services industries, prices and value propositions that were successful yesterday can become outdated or uncompetitive tomorrow.

A commitment to continuous improvement and experimentation in pricing strategies is critical in order to overcome this mistake. That may entail methods such as A/B testing, price elasticity analysis, or customer feedback loops, along with an ability to change or pivot based on new data and insights. By remaining nimble and responsive to changes in the market and customer preferences, you'll ensure that your pricing strategies are at all times up-to-date, effective, and profitable.

It's fair to state that pricing is a challenging and multi-dimensional discipline that requires a profound understanding of customer value, competition dynamics, and market trends. By avoiding these eight common mistakes and embracing a data-oriented, customer-centric pricing approach, technology and services firms can achieve new levels of growth, profitability, and competitiveness in today's dynamic and shifting business environment.

CHAPTER 10: CRITICAL TAKEAWAYS AND FUTURE TRENDS

We have deeply explored the complex, ever-changing pricing landscape in the technology and services sectors. We have looked at how companies can make pricing work to their advantage and trigger sustainable, long-term growth, with value-based pricing as its centerpiece. We have understood how pricing leaders have generated millions of dollars of wealth for their businesses, their workers, and their stockholders. We have taken energy from the revolutionary capacity of AI and machine learning to remake the practice of pricing. We have received the insight and kindness of the World Champion Sponsors and Lead Sponsors who shared their tales with us.

When we return from our journey, a moment of reflection is useful. As we look back over the interviews and case histories we have been reporting in these pages, some overriding lessons and conclusions emerge. By distilling those lessons into a set of best practices – a roadmap – we can offer technology and services companies a valuable tool to make pricing a profound driver of performance and keep them ahead of the structural curve in an increasingly competitive and fluid market.

Lesson 1: Adopt a Customer-Centric Mindset At its core, a major theme that emerges from our discussion on pricing strategies is the concept of incorporating the customer into every decision. By using value-based pricing, segmentation and differentiation, or offerings tailored to specific customers, the most successful companies are able to focus on and meet the distinct needs, tastes, and willingness to pay off specific groups.

To create a pricing approach focused on the customer, companies need to invest in thorough market research, data analytics, customer feedback mechanisms, and optimization algorithms. This can require creating tools like customer journey mappings, sentiment analysis, and conjoint analysis, and a commitment to continuously testing, learning, and adapting based on real-world data and results.

Lesson 2: Leverage Data and Technology

To be successful in an age filled with digital, companies need to leverage data and technology in their pricing strategies. The power of big data, machine learning, A/B testing, dynamic pricing, etc. can give companies a significant competitive edge in their markets.

To unlock the full potential of data-driven pricing, organizations must develop a culture of experimentation, innovation, and continuous improvement. That may mean investing in new skills and talent, building robust and scalable data infrastructure, and fostering interdepartmental collaboration between pricing, marketing, sales, and technology teams.

Lesson 3: we learn about finding the delicate balance between making a profit and keeping your customers. Making profits is the point of pricing strategy. Maximizing both profit and growth are the goals of the pricing strategies. Striking the wrong balance could deter growth in the future and customers to leave.

In order to strike this balance, companies need to use a comprehensive, strategic approach to pricing that encompasses the entire customer lifecycle and value proposition. That may mean techniques like loyalty programs, bundling and cross-selling, or value-added services that enhance the overall customer experience and encourage long-term retention and advocacy.

Lesson 4: Embrace the Fluid Book Market: Finally, maybe the most critical lesson for companies selling digital books and their services in today's hyperkinetic and resourceful business environment is the receptiveness to transitioning market dynamics and customers' needs. With each new entrant, each new technology, and each new twist to the consumer's whims, the company to sustain its profit will be the one that can adeptly reconfigure its pricing strategy.

In order to encourage this flexibility, businesses will have to create an environment centered around ongoing education, trial and error, and creativity. This could mean regularly revising and trying out pricing structures, examining different combinations of products and features, or educating employees about trends and technologies shaping the field. Staying informed of the newest developments and adopting the most promising approaches to pricing will enable businesses to stay on the cutting edge and continuously identify and exploit new opportunities.

As we gaze into the crystal ball of technology and services industry pricing, one thing is clear: The pace of change and innovation will only accelerate. With artificial intelligence (AI) and automation on the horizon, subscription-based models taking hold, and usage-based models maturing, companies that can stay ahead of the learning curve and agile in the face of new paradigms and technologies will be best positioned to achieve their growth ambitions in the years to come.

At the same time, the foundational concepts and key approaches we explore in this book will be as relevant and important as ever. Based on our own research and consulting, thinking from leading lights in the field, and the latest academic literature, we tease out which pricing strategies, capabilities, and organizational muscles matter most depending on the specifics of the situation. While many of the examples and stories we recount are from the years leading up to the COVID-19 pandemic, the lessons they convey—about the links between value, pricing, and profitability—have staying power. The external economic and operating environment may have shifted, but pricing as an enabler of profit remains just as valid.

Ultimately, what will determine companies' success in pricing won't just be the specific tools, techniques, or models they adopt. It will be the broader culture and mindset they foster around pricing as a strategic and cross-functional discipline. By taking a holistic, customer-centric, and data-driven approach to pricing, and by cultivating a culture of experimentation, collaboration, and continual improvement, technology and services companies can position themselves for sustainable growth and competitive advantage in today's volatile and complex market.

ACKNOWLEDGEMENT

In the creation of this seminal series, I have had the distinct privilege of drawing upon the invaluable experiences, insights, and expertise generously shared by a distinguished global network of esteemed partners and accomplished friends. Their direct and indirect contributions have been instrumental, and it is with profound gratitude that I acknowledge the indelible influence they have had on this work.

Kanth Krishnan: Managing Director at Accenture, has been a beacon of inspiration with his incisive insights and visionary leadership in technology services. His profound depth of knowledge and innovative approach have significantly enriched the content of this book.

As Managing Director at Newmark, Jeff Pappas has provided critical perspectives on the dynamic global real estate market landscape. His unparalleled expertise has contributed to a deeper understanding of the business environments explored herein.

Haitao Qi, Chairman of Devott Research and Advisory, has provided exceptionally enlightening perspectives on technology innovations and market trends, especially in the Asian context.

Formerly leading Outsourcing and Managed Services at PwC, Charles Aird's comprehensive knowledge and strategic foresight in outsourcing services have greatly contributed to my understanding of this critical business function.

It has been my great privilege to learn from and collaborate with these distinguished individuals and institutions operating at the leading edge of our industry. Any merits of this book stem directly from the exceptional global network of friends and partners upon whom I rely. Any faults or shortcomings are solely my own.

Last but not least, the unwavering understanding and support of my beloved wife, Biyu, has been an inspiration to this professional endeavor. The intensive writing workload harkened back to my doctoral dissertation at Yale a quarter-century ago. She remains the driving force behind my career growth and personal fulfillment.

ABOUT THE AUTHOR

Stephan S. Sunn

Stephan Sunn is the Executive Partner at Sanford Black Advisory, a preeminent global business and investment consultancy. In this capacity, he collaborates with industry leaders to advise companies worldwide on growth strategy, marketing/sales, innovation monetization, partnerships, and mergers & acquisitions. Over the past two decades, Mr. Sunn has consulted on sourcing provider selection for more than 30 international corporations and over 20 investment and M&A deals in the technology services, digital technologies, and global outsourcing sectors.

Mr. Sunn possesses particular expertise in empowering private enterprises to accelerate growth and enhance value creation through engagement with governments and technology parks. He holds a leadership position with Devott Co., China's largest private research firm focused on the IT, software, and technology services industries. Additionally, he serves as a Director at the China IT and Outsourcing Association. His clients span Fortune 500 companies, state-owned enterprises, technology parks, SMBs, and startups in both developed and emerging markets.

A graduate of the University of Science and Technology of China (USTC) with a Bachelor of Science degree, and Yale University with a Master of Science and Ph.D., Mr. Sunn frequently shares his insights and research as a speaker at global conferences and events. He is a prolific author and an accomplished presenter for his projects and clients around the world.

BOOKS BY THIS AUTHOR

Competing For The Growth

This book serves as a guidebook for city planners, economic development professionals, tech park builders, and public officials who aim to create thriving innovation communities that attract global trade and stimulate investments. It offers a structured path that begins with intangible factors like vision setting and partnership alignment and extends to pilots and full-blown magnet programs.

The book provides real-life instructions to help put these ideas into practice, including effective strategies for attracting rapidly growing businesses and talent, creating a setting that promotes innovation and entrepreneurship, fostering a competitive and appealing business climate, and building a globally recognized brand and reputation.

The author emphasizes that cities and tech parks must play to their strengths and assets to compete and win in the global arena. The race for relevance is on, and the window of opportunity to determine the outcome is closing. Cities and companies have what they need to succeed, and with the options, relationships, and guidance provided in this book, city managers and tech park authorities can make the decisions necessary to lead their communities to success in the world investment and trade arena.

Searching The New Profits

In the face of global market turbulence and domestic uncertainties, American small and medium-sized businesses (SMBs) and startups have significant growth opportunities in emerging markets. However, these markets also present unique challenges. This handbook provides a semi-analytical and semi-prescriptive approach to help American SMBs and entrepreneurs succeed in these rapidly expanding markets. Conversely, governments, technology parks, and corporations in emerging countries can utilize this book to learn how to collaborate with U.S. companies in their markets to serve their customers effectively.

The book covers essential themes such as researching and identifying matching markets, choosing the appropriate market entry mode, local marketing and sales tactics, effective risk management, establishing an active and reputable presence in the local market, ensuring full legal compliance, avoiding political involvement, talent search and retention, and balancing standardization and localization. The final chapter shares valuable lessons from decades of business practices, acknowledging that readers may have different perspectives on these topics. Expanding knowledge through diverse viewpoints is beneficial for U.S. SMB and startup leaders. Despite the challenges, penetrating foreign markets can be highly profitable, and U.S. enterprises have a reasonable chance of success by capitalizing on the vast potential of these rapidly growing territories.

Cracking The Winning Codes

This book serves as a comprehensive guide for international technology and outsourcing companies seeking to enter and succeed in the highly competitive U.S. market. It emphasizes the importance of adapting to the unique American business culture, which values innovation, diversity, relationships, customer-centricity, and results-oriented management. The guide highlights the need to navigate the complex U.S. regulatory landscape, including federal and state laws, as well as key legislations such as FCPA, SOX, and HIPAA.

The book covers essential topics such as understanding American business culture, complying with legal requirements, developing effective marketing strategies, employing successful sales techniques, addressing cultural differences, and managing risks associated with entering a new market.

Additionally, it encourages the use of innovative tactics to differentiate from competitors and gain market share.

A special section titled "The Lessons" shares the author's personal experiences and insights, providing practical execution tips that focus on solution-oriented approaches, leveraging referrals and testimonials, managing communication costs, delivering higher quality than promised, and investing in proven local sales leaders.

By adhering to the core principles of understanding buyer preferences, continuous innovation, human capital development, risk management, customer-centricity, and resilient operations, global providers can successfully navigate and thrive in the lucrative U.S. market.

Win More Businesses

In the digital age, businesses must navigate the complex landscape of Marketing Technology (Martech) and Sales Technology (Salestech) to stay competitive and drive growth. "Win More Deals in Global Markets" provides a comprehensive guide for leveraging these technologies to enhance customer experiences, streamline processes, and boost revenue across international markets. The book explores the convergence of marketing, sales, and technology, emphasizing the importance of data-driven decision-making and cross-functional collaboration. It offers strategies for overcoming challenges in digital transformation, such as resistance to change and skills gaps, while also addressing the unique considerations of global expansion and localization.
The authors predict future trends in Martech and Salestech, including the increasing role of AI, personalization, and emerging technologies like AR/VR and voice interfaces. Through real-world success stories from global brands like Coca-Cola, Sephora, and Airbnb, readers gain valuable insights into harnessing the power of these technologies for business success. This book serves as an essential resource for executives and professionals seeking to navigate the digital ecosystem and drive growth in the international marketplace.

Renovations Or Revolutions

The book "Renovation or Revolution? Impacts of Latest AI on BPO and Contact-centers Industries" provides an in-depth exploration of the transformative potential of artificial intelligence (AI) within the business process outsourcing (BPO) and contact center industries. It emphasizes the importance of early adoption, customization, and localization of AI solutions to gain a competitive edge in the global marketplace. The book highlights the evolving role of human agents, who will focus on complex problem-solving and relationship-building, while AI handles routine tasks. It also discusses the development of AI expertise within organizations and the ethical considerations surrounding AI implementation.

The authors present a roadmap for incorporating AI, underlining the need for a clear vision, employee training, and continuous improvement. Looking ahead, the book envisions a future of collaborative human-AI partnerships, hyper-personalization, and proactive customer engagement. It stresses that embracing AI is crucial for BPO and contact center companies to achieve sustainable growth and remain competitive in the international arena. The book serves as a comprehensive guide for executives navigating the AI revolution in the global business services industry.

Risky Reefs In The Ocean Of Global Markets

This book provides a comprehensive roadmap for emerging market companies venturing into global expansion. It highlights common pitfalls across strategic planning, finance, operations, human resources, marketing, technology, legal/ethics, and risk management. The book emphasizes thorough market research, cultural adaptation, local partnerships, brand building, innovation investment, and long-term vision.
As the global landscape evolves, it anticipates trends like digitization, sustainability integration, and talent acquisition challenges. The book provides corporate decision-makers with insights and best practices to navigate complexities, mitigate risks, and foster sustainable growth while driving innovation and progress internationally.

The AI Revolution In B2B Marketing And Sales

This professional guidance provides a comprehensive playbook for leveraging artificial intelligence (AI) to drive measurable results in B2B marketing and sales strategies. With insights from real-world case studies spanning diverse industries and business sizes, it explores AI's transformative impact on understanding the AI-empowered buyer, delivering personalized omnichannel experiences, boosting sales productivity, and optimizing operations.

The book offers a strategic framework for successful AI implementation, covering data readiness, talent acquisition, governance, and ethical considerations. Globally applicable principles foster human-AI collaboration, enabling organizations worldwide to harness AI's potential ethically and profitably in the B2B domain.

www.ingramcontent.com/pod-product-compliance
Lightning Source LLC
Chambersburg PA
CBHW072054230526
45479CB00010B/1061